# MARRIAGE
## AND
# CHILDREN

[
Marriage and Finances
Children, Teens, and Money
]

MONEYLIFE™ BASICS SERIES

ISBN 978-1-56427-255-3

*For inquiries in Canada, please contact CrownCanada.ca or call 1-866-401-0626.*

August 2008 Edition

# CONTENTS

# INTRODUCTION

God's first command to newly created man and woman was *"Be fruitful and multiply"* (Genesis 1:28). This has never ceased to be among our highest priorities.

Marriage, as our closest relationship, usually offers our greatest relationship rewards and challenges. Not surprisingly, how we handle money within this relationship is vitally important because it reflects our heart.

Training our children to understand the importance of handling money wisely—including money's inability to provide the fulfillment that comes only when our relationship with God is our highest priority—is one of the greatest gifts we can give them.

This book will help you if you:

- are married or considering marriage,

- have children or grandchildren,

- are responsible for the care of children, or

- want to understand and help someone in one of these categories.

The first section addresses areas that should be explored prior to marriage. If you are already married, please don't think this section is not for you. Many people who have been married for decades have not yet understood each other's background, perspective, values, and money-handling patterns. Take your time here.

The time you invest in this small book and its associated resources could change the quality of the rest of your life—and your children's lives.

You may be in a state of financial crisis. There is hope for you. Millions of us can attest to discovering the freedom of financial faithfulness as we have applied these principles found in God's Word. You shouldn't expect a quick fix, but you can expect a steady, progressive transformation of your finances—and life. With God, you can be confident that even if you experience a crisis, it need not be a tragedy.

And if you're not in a state of crisis, thank God for the privilege of getting things in order so that you can avoid one—at least one of your own making. If God permits a crisis in spite of your prudent stewardship, you can trust Him to redeem it as He guides you and strengthens you through it.

### *Help and Hope Are Here.*

***Crown exists to provide help, hope, and insight.*** These Help and Hope buttons appear whenever special information is available to assist and encourage you.

Please notice a few helpful features we include in every *MoneyLife™ Basics Series* book.

1. Appendix 1 is an introduction to Christ. If you (or someone you know) are uncertain about where you stand with God, this short introduction will guide you into an intimate relationship with Him.

2. Appendix 2, "God's Ownership & Financial Faithfulness,"

briefly explores a fundamental concept—one that frames the correct perspective on every financial principle in Scripture. If you don't understand this, you are likely to manage your resources with worldly wisdom. The world's approach to money management isn't always evil, but it is short-sighted (ignoring eternity), incomplete (ignoring the Creator/Controller/Provider), and usually in pursuit of the wrong goals.

3. Because we are committed to transformation rather than mere information, each chapter ends with a two-part exercise:

- An Action Step you create based on your response to the chapter

- A Celebration Plan for every Action Step completed

Please take advantage of these to maximize your experience in this small book. James 1:22 sums it up when it says, *"Do not merely listen to the word, and so deceive yourselves. Do what it says"* (NIV).

# CHAPTER 1

# MARRIAGE AND FINANCES

## *Section 1: Getting Acquainted*

This section, although directed toward people anticipating marriage, is appropriate for those who are already married as well. Whether you use it as a review and refresher or as a means of discovering things about each other that you missed in your preparation for marriage (We've all missed a lot!), you will find it well worth every minute you give it.

The engagement period preceding marriage is filled with busy preparations, one of which is confirming whether God has led you to spend the rest of your life with your intended partner. Since the values you each bring to the marriage relationship are crucial components, now is the time to discover and discuss them.

Jesus taught that money management is an outward indicator of a person's spiritual life and values. *"For where your treasure is, there your heart will be also"* (Matthew 6:21). By examining your patterns of handling money, as well as those of your future mate, you can discover important lifestyle traits like these.

- Selfishness versus cooperation
- Pride versus humility
- Greed versus generosity
- Deliberate/planning versus spontaneous/disorganization
- Decision–making style
- Conflict management/how you handle disagreements
- Trusting God versus independence

The following exercises are designed to help the two of you become better acquainted with the values you associate with money and wealth.

## Food for Thought

1. Suppose you receive a surprise wedding gift of $10,000. Working separately, outline a plan of what you would do with the money. Then compare your plans, being careful to explore the values underlying them. How were your plans alike? How did they differ?

2. Take turns discussing what you each learned about money management from your parents. What good habits did they have that you intend to keep in your marriage?

   How will your money management habits be different from those of your parents? Discuss your answers with your partner, and be careful to explore your views.

3. Below is a series of factors that frequently have a major impact on family finances. Share with your partner the importance of each factor to your marriage.

- Home ownership
- Driving late model cars
- Education
- Having children
- Wearing name-brand clothing
- Faithful tithing
- Health insurance
- New furniture
- Choosing where to live
- One spouse staying home with children

## Going Further

1. Read Luke 12:15-21 and answer this question: Is it possible for a person to be materially rich and spiritually poor? Place a check mark beside the factors that are essential to your definition of wealth. When you are finished, compare your answers to those of your partner.

☐ Size of your bank account

☐ Health

☐ Bible knowledge

☐ Friends

- [ ] Size of your home
- [ ] Academic degrees
- [ ] Year and model of cars
- [ ] Country club membership
- [ ] Understanding your life purpose
- [ ] Church family
- [ ] Occupation or profession
- [ ] Name-brand clothing
- [ ] Eating at restaurants
- [ ] Amount of vacation time
- [ ] Reputation
- [ ] Peace of mind
- [ ] Living in a free nation

2. Every follower of Christ has the privilege of managing the money God has entrusted to him or her. *"You gave them charge of everything you made, putting all things under their authority"* (Psalm 8:6, NLT). *"Now, a person who is put in charge as a manager must be faithful"* (1 Corinthians 4:2, NLT). Individually record your answers to the following questions on a separate sheet of paper. Then, share them with your partner.

   a. What does it mean to you to be a faithful manager?

   b. If being a faithful manager requires knowing what the owner wants, how do we find out?

c. The world trusts money for fulfillment, viewing it as power, social status and emotional security. As faithful managers of God's resources, where is our trust, and how does our view of money differ from the world's?

d. Why do you think it is important, before marriage, to learn to be a good manager of what God gives you?

3. In addition to what you and your partner have studied in this section, it is important that both of you share your attitudes, ideas, and feelings in specific areas of financial responsibility. Discuss with your partner the following areas of personal finances, keeping notes of your conclusions as well as areas where you disagree and need further discussion.

- When to combine bank accounts, titles to vehicles, or homes

- Living on a budget/using a written spending plan

- Who will be the primary caretaker for paying bills and balancing the checkbook

- Career plans

- Investments

- Long-term financial planning

- Life insurance

- Making a will

## Section 2: God's Will in Finances

Discerning and obeying God's will in all matters, including finances, is paramount for every follower of Christ. *"Seek first His kingdom and His righteousness, and all these things will be added to you"* (Matthew 6:33). By serving Jesus Christ first, your needs will be met.

Although you must take responsibility for discerning God's direction in a financial matter (e.g., what house to buy or rent), the Bible provides general guidelines that reflect His will. In the absence of solid biblical teaching, many people conclude that God simply provides money for their pleasures and desires without any purpose or direction for its use. This section reviews fundamental biblical principles for managing money that will maximize your faithfulness to God and allow Him the freedom to use your marriage and your money for His glory.

**Food for Thought**

1. **Honor God with the tithe.** A tithe is 10 percent of your income that is set aside for God's work. Leviticus 27:30 states that the tithe *"is the Lord's; it is holy to the Lord."*

   Throughout your life as a married couple, resist a lifestyle that requires you to spend money that belongs to God. Read Malachi 3:10-11 and summarize here the specific blessings from God to those who tithe.

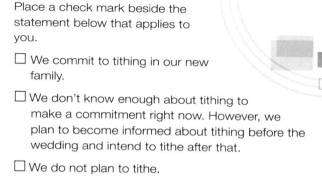

Place a check mark beside the statement below that applies to you.

☐ We commit to tithing in our new family.

☐ We don't know enough about tithing to make a commitment right now. However, we plan to become informed about tithing before the wedding and intend to tithe after that.

☐ We do not plan to tithe.

2. **Avoid get-rich-quick schemes.** A get-rich-quick attitude is risky because it tempts people to live beyond their means, to get involved with things they don't understand sufficiently, and to make hasty decisions. *"The plans of the diligent lead surely to advantage, but everyone who is hasty comes surely to poverty"* (Proverbs 21:5). In the space below, paraphrase 1 Timothy 6:9-10, and give particular attention to the stern warnings given to those who long to be rich materially.

3. **Practice contentment.** Generally speaking, would others describe you as a contented person? *"Make sure that your character is free from the love of money, being content with what you have; for He Himself has*

said, 'I will never desert you, nor will I ever forsake you'"
(Hebrews 13:5). Why do you think God's presence and
promises diminish feelings of discontentment?

### Going Further

4. **Share from your abundance** to meet the needs of
others. The Scripture teaches that God provides a
surplus in order to help meet the needs of others. *"At
this present time your abundance being a supply for
their need, so that their abundance also may become
a supply for your need, that there may be equality"* (2
Corinthians 8:14). State how the following attitudes in
you could obstruct God's plans to use your surplus to
meet the needs of others.

   a. Fear

   b. Pride

   c. Greed

5. **Practice saving.** Every family should set aside
between three and six month's net income as
an emergency surplus. These resources can
be used to pay for unexpected expenses,
such as car repairs or illnesses. *"Go to
the ant, O sluggard, observe her ways*

*and be wise, which, having no chief, officer or ruler, prepares her food in the summer and gathers her provision in the harvest"* (Proverbs 6:6-8). What percentage of your income do you intend to save each month after your wedding?

_____ percent

6. **Pay back what you owe.** Although the Bible doesn't teach that borrowing is a sin, neither does it speak of it in a positive light. If you borrow, the clear teaching of Scripture is to pay back what you owe. *"The wicked borrows and does not pay back, but the righteous is gracious and gives"* (Psalm 37:21). Why do you think it is so important to God that you repay all that you have borrowed?

Regardless of poor decisions that you have made in the past or the current status of your finances, God's mercy and wisdom is available every day to start and continue a new plan that involves Him. Take the next positive step in your journey together—you can trust Him!

## Section 3: Using Credit and Credit Cards

A simple law of physics states that what goes up must come down. Translated to the world of credit, the principle could be stated like this: What gets borrowed must be paid back. Yet consider these startling facts about the abuse of credit in America.

- One in three Christian adults say they cannot get ahead due to the financial debt they have incurred.

- Ninety percent of all personal bankruptcies are due to out-of-control credit card debt.

- The fastest-growing segment of the credit card industry is consumers who are least equipped to carry debt loads—young people and those with lower incomes.

- Less than 50 percent of cardholders typically pay off their balance in full at the end of each month.

Credit cards should be required to have a warning label affixed: "Caution: Credit cards may be hazardous to your marriage!" Are you prepared to handle credit wisely so that it won't become a divisive issue in your marriage?

**Food for Thought**

1. God's Word neither prohibits nor encourages borrowing. Do you and your intended partner plan to use credit? Discuss with each other your reasons why or why not.

2. Many banks offer an overdraft protection feature that includes a line of credit. If offered this feature, do you

plan to use it? What problems
could potentially occur if you do?

3. Use the space below to list each debt you will
   bring into the marriage, including both the balance due
   and monthly payment. If you need more space, use
   another sheet of paper.

### Husband's Debts

| Creditor | Balance | Monthly Payment |
|---|---|---|
|  |  |  |
|  |  |  |
|  |  |  |

### Wife's Debts

| Creditor | Balance | Monthly Payment |
|---|---|---|
|  |  |  |
|  |  |  |
|  |  |  |

## Going Further

1. How does Proverbs 22:7 describe the relationship
   between a borrower and lender? Record your answer
   below to seal it in your memory.

2. Study the following Scripture verses, and note what each teaches about the financial responsibility of a married couple.

- Proverbs 3:27-28

- Proverbs 21:20

- Ecclesiastes 5:4-5

- James 4:13-16

3. Credit cards are not the real culprit; abuse of credit cards is. To prevent this abuse that has led to so much heartache, we suggest you abide by the three simple rules below. Place your initials next to each rule that you will agree to follow.

**Rules for Using Credit Cards**

1. Use credit cards to purchase only budgeted items. If you're not living on a spending plan, do not use credit cards.

2. Pay the balance in full for each credit card every month.

3. The first time you cannot pay your balances in full, cut up your cards and throw them away. You've begun the slippery slide into living beyond your means.

The slide can be relatively pain-less while additional credit remains available, but the landing is far from painless. Postponing the inevitable just makes the hole deeper and the solution more painful. The stress can be a killer even if you manage to avoid bank-ruptcy.

For more information on credit card debt and how to reduce the potential burden of debt in your finances, check out some other resources available from Crown or your local bookstore:

- *Free and Clear* by Howard Dayton (ISBN 0-8024-2257-8)

- *Your Money Map* by Howard Dayton (ISBN 0-8024-6869-1)

- *MoneyLife™ Basics Series – Debt and Bankruptcy* (ISBN 978-1-56427-251-5)

## Section 4: How to Establish a Spending Plan

A spending plan can help you control spending and arrange your expenses to fulfill God's purposes. This disciplined ap-proach will result in greater satisfaction, fewer financial prob-lems, and greater financial stability for your family. Under the lordship of Jesus Christ, you will control your money instead of having it control you.

Seek God's guidance as you set up your spending plan. *"The mind of man plans his way, but the Lord directs his steps"*

(Proverbs 16:9). To begin this section, discuss the following questions:

- Which expenses are essential?

- Which items can you do without?

- Which expenses can you reduce?

## Food for Thought

1. It is important for a prospective mate to learn how to manage his or her money prior to marriage. Do you agree or disagree? Do you presently use a written spending plan?

2. Marriage often attracts opposites, including opposite tendencies for handling money. One of you is likely to overspend, the other is more likely to hoard. Place your initials beside the tendency that best describes you. Does your mate agree with your assessment?

_____ overspending        _____ hoarding

3. Taken to the extreme, either overspending or hoarding can lead to great heartache in your marriage. Study the Scripture passages below to determine what God says to correct each tendency.

### *Overspending*

- Proverbs 23:4-5

- Matthew 6:19-24

- 1 Timothy 6:7-10

### *Hoarding*

- Ecclesiastes 5:13

- Luke 12:15

- 2 Corinthians 9:6-7

4. How will a spending plan help to restrain an over-spender? How will a spending plan enable a hoarder to become more generous?

### Going Further

Use the percentages below to develop your first spending plan. These guidelines will enable you to meet your obligations, tithe to God's work, consistently save money, and still not over-spend. Because spending patterns will vary based on income level and size of the family, the percentages shown (based on a $35,000 gross income) should be regarded only as estimates.

Visit our Web site at Crown.org for free access to Crown's online spending plan calculator. This convenient tool automatically calculates the dollar amounts for each spending plan category based on income and giving pattern.

# Percentage Guide

| Gross Income | $25,000 | 35,000 | 45,000 | 55,000 | 85,000 | 115,000 |
|---|---|---|---|---|---|---|
| 1. Tithe/Giving | 10% | 10% | 10% | 10% | 10% | 10% |
| 2. Taxes[1] | *2.7% | 11.2% | 14.8% | 17.2% | 23.5% | 26.3% |
| **Net Spendable Income** | **$21,825** | **27,580** | **33,840** | **40,040** | **58,475** | **73,255** |
| 3. Housing | 39% | 36% | 32% | 30% | 30% | 29% |
| 4. Food | 15% | 12% | 13% | 12% | 11% | 11% |
| 5. Transportation | 15% | 12% | 13% | 14% | 13% | 13% |
| 6. Insurance | 5% | 5% | 5% | 5% | 5% | 5% |
| 7. Debts | 5% | 5% | 5% | 5% | 5% | 5% |
| 8. Entertainment/Recreation | 3% | 5% | 5% | 7% | 7% | 8% |
| 9. Clothing | 4% | 5% | 5% | 6% | 7% | 7% |
| 10. Savings | 5% | 5% | 5% | 5% | 5% | 5% |
| 11. Medical/Dental | 5% | 6% | 6% | 5% | 5% | 5% |
| 12. Miscellaneous | 4% | 4% | 6% | 6% | 7% | 7% |
| 13. Investments[2] | – | 5% | 5% | 5% | 5% | 5% |
| If you have school/child care expenses, these percentages must be deducted from other categories. | | | | | | |
| 14. School/Child Care[3] | 8% | 6% | 5% | 5% | 5% | 5% |

[1] Guideline percentages for tax category include taxes for Social Security, federal, and a small estimated amount for state, based on 2002 rates. The tax code changes regularly. Please be sure to insert your actual tax into this category.

[2] This category is used for long-term investment planning, such as college education or retirement.

[3] This category is added as a guide only. If you have this expense, the percentage shown must be deducted from other spending plan categories.

* In some cases earned income credit will apply. It may be possible to increase the number of deductions to lessen the amount of tax paid per month. Review the last tax return for specific information.

**Note:** The Percentage Guide is based on a married couple with two children.

*Single adults* should adjust the Percentage Guide as follows: Food 10-14%, Transportation 12-15%, Insurance 4%, Debts 5%, Entertainment/Recreation 6-8%, Clothing 5-7%, Savings 5-7%, Medical/Dental 5%, Miscellaneous 4-7%, Investments 5%, and School 0-7%. Housing remains the same unless you have roommates. If you have roommates, reduce Housing to 25% and add the Housing surplus to the other categories.

*Single parents* should adjust the Percentage Guide as follows: Food 12-14%, Transportation 12-14%, Insurance 3-4%, Entertainment/Recreation 3-4%, Clothing 5-6%, and Miscellaneous 3-4%. The Percentage Guides for the other categories will remain the same.

### *Spending Plan Goals*

Place your initials beside each goal upon which you both agree.

_____ 1. We agree to live on a written spending plan.

_____ 2. We agree to balance our checkbook to the penny every month.

_____ 3. We agree to begin setting aside at least a small amount every month toward an emergency surplus fund until it equals three to six month's income.

_____ 4. If we use credit cards, we agree to pay off the balances each month or stop using the cards altogether.

_____ 5. We agree to live within our means.

_____ 6. We agree to save something every month.

_____ 7. We agree to tithe to God's work.

For more information on creating a successful spending plan, choose any of the following resources available at Crown.org/BudgetingSolutions:

- Family Budgeting Package (Crown's Paper Budgeting Solution)

- *Crown Money Map™ Financial Software* (Crown's Software Budgeting Solution)

- *Crown™ Mvelopes® Personal* (Crown's Online and Mobile Budgeting Solution)

## Section 5: Communication and Finances

When you marry, you voluntarily commit yourselves to each other as partners for life, binding your futures together. This unwavering commitment thrives on trusting each other's intent and communicating carefully to maintain clear understanding. Marriage is no place for secrets or deceit.

Studying God's Word together, praying together, and even managing your money together are spiritual exercises that contribute to a strong marriage.

As you read through this section, be honest in sharing your insights and feelings with your partner. Make a mutual commitment to follow through with your decisions. Agree to hold each other accountable for meeting your financial goals, and devise a plan for regular evaluation of how well you are succeeding. *"Two are better than one because they have a good return for their labor. For if either of them falls, the one will lift up his companion. But woe to the one who falls when there is not another to lift him up"* (Ecclesiastes 4:9-10).

The questions below will help you discuss important family matters.

### Food for Thought

1. It is important to have joint bank accounts—both checking and savings. Do you agree or disagree? Share your reasons with each other.

2. One area of marriage that carries important financial consequences is that of having children. Do you plan to have children? If so, do you agree (generally)

on the ideal circumstances for having children? Will one parent remain at home with the child? Discuss your viewpoints thoroughly.

3. Another important area is church attendance. Have the two of you agreed where you will attend?

☐ Yes    ☐ No

What qualities are important to you in a church family?

4. Which of the following describes how you plan to spend your first Christmas Day as a married couple? If already married, how do you discuss and agree on such plans?

a. We will spend Christmas Day alone—just the two of us!

b. We will spend Christmas Day with friends.

c. We will spend Christmas Day with the wife's extended family.

d. We will spend Christmas Day with the husband's extended family.

e. Another plan (Describe below).

5. How much do you plan to spend on your honeymoon/ next major vacation? $ _____

Do you plan to pay for it with

☐ cash?    ☐ credit cards?

☐ combination of both?    ☐ other?

If you use credit cards during the honeymoon/vacation, how much do you expect to owe when you return home?  $ _____

**Going Further**

Describe why the teaching in each verse below will be important for good communication in your marriage.

1. Romans 12:14-18

2. Ephesians 4:25

3. Ephesians 4:26-27

4. Ephesians 5:4

It is crucial for you to clearly communicate your financial plans and goals to each other prior to marriage and stick to them after marriage. Challenge yourselves to follow through on the commitments you have made as a result of this study. You will be so thankful that you have planned ahead for future decisions like the ones listed above.

**Remember:** Money decisions are a daily part of married life. Nothing you do affects you alone; every decision involves your partner's welfare as well as your own. To discover the joy of saving and spending what God has entrusted to you, seek His wisdom. With each decision and every step of follow-through, you are strengthening the base for a successful and fulfilling lifelong partnership. God will give you the wisdom and ability to be successful in your marriage and finances as you seek Him!

### Leading a Life Group
**Tom and Barbara Wiedenbeck's Story**

As life group leaders in Wisconsin's capital city, Tom and Barbara Wiedenbeck have taught a broad range of couples and parents.

When asked for a sampling of their students, Barbara replied, "Single parents, retirees, middle-agers, et cetera. One older couple was concerned because they wanted to retire soon and their financial house was not wholly in order. One single mom had spent too much of her life in an immoral occupation. But now, she's on track morally and spiritually and wants to pull things together even more.

"One young couple didn't seem to like each other when they started in the group, due to hard situations they'd been through. Over the course of the study, they grasped biblical principles that helped them appreciate each other. They began paying down their debts and were a different couple by the time the study ended."

## The benefits of submission

"For us, the Crown life groups have been sort of a microcosm of the big, broad world that's out there," Barbara says.

They have noticed that just as their students have come from a wide variety of backgrounds, God moves in their lives in a wide variety of ways—according to specific needs—when they submit to Him.

"Part of the reason the Crown study is so effective is that it helps people pay attention to God in their personal, detailed, everyday lives," Barbara says. "It is life-changing, and Tom is always impressed with how quickly people's lives are affected. I've also noticed in these studies that God often puts people with similar situations and issues together, which leads to bonding and support—even in cases in which you might not expect it to happen."

## More than finances

One reason Tom continues teaching the study is that he sees its impact on character, not just finances. "Character affects the totality of your life," he says. "The impact of the study filters into people's relationships, workplace, and church life as well as into their checkbooks and credit card statements. It impacts their overall understanding of God and the lives He wants for us."

Marriages and families are among the biggest beneficiaries of improved priorities.

### Raising sheep: Examples from God's Word

As a couple, Tom and Barbara combine differing interests and abilities into their home and work life. From a farm in Oregon, Wisconsin, Tom operates an electrical contracting business with several employees while Barbara oversees a flock of sheep and one "token" llama.

"Some people buy a Miata or Jag when they hit mid-life," she jokes. "We bought sheep! It is really calming to look out the window and see them there."

The Wiedenbecks see many of the Bible's object lessons concerning sheep played out before them.

"The Lord talks about shepherding and compares us to sheep," Barbara says. "They aren't the dumbest creatures on earth, but they do some dumb, follow-the-crowd things at times. So, there are scriptural lessons that come to life in our pastures."

"Sometimes sheep are happy with the shepherd and follow directions, going where they are supposed to go," Tom says. "At other times you try to lead or push them to another pasture with better grass, but they keep returning to the same worn-out pasture where they have been.

"They struggle and fight the shepherd, even though the shepherd knows what is best for them and puts it right in front of their noses!"

### Teaching children to follow God's plan

From the beginning of their marriage 25 years ago, Tom and Barbara listened to Crown's radio programs and studied what the Bible says about money. And they passed it on to their four children.

"We followed Larry Burkett's guideline of 10-50-40," Barbara says. "Kids should tithe, save half of the total, and then spend the rest. It's worked very well.

"All our children give above the tithe and have savings accounts. They enjoy serving at church and helping with individuals in need, both here and abroad."

At a time when there is so much negative publicity about young people, the four Wiedenbeck children provide an encouraging reminder of what can happen when adults incorporate God's principles, financial and otherwise, into their parenting.

Ranging in age from late teens to mid-20s, these young adults exhibit an eagerness to give and serve. It is evident in their choices—from extracurricular activities to college majors to career paths to church and ministry involvement.

"We're entering our 21st year of home education this fall," Barbara says. "We hope our kids have learned some biblical lessons from us or from the outside arenas we've placed them in or encouraged them to pursue.

"We've always felt that the most effective teaching or example is the way you live your life. That says a lot more than whatever we would tell our kids. If what we're living is not what we're telling them, then the words won't make any difference anyway." ■

## *Your Response*

### So what do I do now?

We encourage you to write at least one Action Step in response to the chapter you have just read. If you write more than one, prioritize them in a logical order so you have a clear first step that you can begin immediately.

### *Action Steps* _____

_____

_____

_____

_____

_____

_____

_____

We also encourage you to reward yourself for every Action Step completed. Since the enemy ("the accuser") will discourage you by making the journey seem impossibly long, you need to see each step as its own victory. Your progress will be faster and more enjoyable if you take a little time to celebrate it.

Your celebration doesn't have to take a lot of time or money to be meaningful. Just make it something you enjoy, and tie it to the Action Step you have completed.

## *Celebration Plan*

# CHAPTER 2

# FINANCES FOR CHILDREN AND TEENS

## *Section 1: What Went Wrong, What We Can Do*

Consumer overspending. Record numbers of personal bankruptcies. Huge government deficits.

With so many people suffering from financial problems these days, we want to believe tomorrow's leaders and consumers will do a better job of managing their money. But are they headed down the same road their parents took?

That question was on the minds of researchers who decided to test the consumer knowledge of 428 high school seniors in eight metropolitan areas. When the results were tabulated, the teenagers' average score for the entire test was only 42 percent.

This doesn't mean there's no hope for the future. In fact, many parents still have an opportunity to influence their children; reading this book is a first step toward achieving that goal.

However, before we discuss teaching our children, let's do a brief review of history to see how today's attitudes about money developed.

## What Went Wrong

Prior to the 1920s, many people worked on farms. They had to manage their money well because, for the most part, they had nowhere to go for help in case of trouble.

The family's budgeting system might have consisted of nothing more than large canning jars labeled "Food," "Clothing," "Medical," and so on. The family finances were neither complex nor mysterious, and most children had a feel for what was going on.

In contrast, children today may not be sure what their parents do for a living. When the parents buy groceries, the children may not be around. And if the parents are having financial difficulties, the children may not know. After all, parents reason, it would just upset them and, for the time being, Mom and Dad can live off their credit cards.

This change from a direct correlation between work, money, and goods to a less visible relationship between them, has had a great impact. Even the immediate connection between work and money is gone.

We've lost track of the value of our money. When we sign our names on credit slips, it doesn't seem like we're spending real money, and right at the moment we're not. But reality sets in when we're still making payments on an item that has broken, worn out, or lost its thrill.

When we work hard and sacrifice in order to save for the things we want, we have time to make informed, time-tempered decisions. We have a real understanding of the value of each dollar, and we want to get the best value for our hard-earned money.

Likewise, when we teach our children how to plan and save—to fulfill their goals—they are less prone to emotional, impulse buying. They see the results and feel good about themselves and the decisions they have made.

## Want Versus Wait

Let's look back in history again. Imagine a family seated around the dinner table, where the children are discussing what they want to be when they grow up.

They know they have to work hard, develop their skills, and learn to earn their way in life. In the meantime, they make do with what is available, whether it be homegrown, bartered, or hand-me-down.

Today, there are all sorts of government programs to help us achieve our goals and catch us when we fall. And when it comes to college, there are government loans. Unfortunately, there is not enough thought about the payments that will be required when those loans come due.

The same is true of other payments, including those on homes, cars, and credit cards. These days you can get 90-year loans. In Japan, three-generation loans are available!

Even worse, banks, government, and merchants look for more ways to extend credit. In the 1950s a person could not qualify for a credit card unless he or she had a very healthy salary. Now credit cards are given to high school students.

These practices are accepted because people have become accustomed to living on assumed wealth, rather than earned wealth. Through the use of credit, people buy things they can't afford to own so they can have them now.

What happened to working hard, saving, investing wisely, and managing money?

Unfortunately, many people are relying on the remote possibility that they will become rich overnight. For example, consider how people answered the survey question, "How does a person become successful?"

- Win the lottery.
- Think of a great product idea and sell a million of them.
- Become a rock star.
- Become a famous actor.
- Get into professional sports.
- Get into the stock market.

### Get It Now!

One of the biggest culprits in today's attitudes about money is advertising. When it began, advertising's purpose was to tell us about the benefits of certain products so that if we needed them, we could make an informed choice.

But the message changed from simply telling us about products to trying to convince us we needed products we'd never heard of before. Instead of "find a need and fill it," it became "create a need and fill it."

What is advertising's message? As long as you have credit available, your financial state is irrelevant. Satisfy your desires. You deserve it! Who needs cash when credit works just as well? Get it now!

## More Money

Also affecting today's attitudes about money are the media, which exalt the huge salaries drawn by professional athletes, actors, and musicians. According to society, these people have it made. Or do they?

The fact is, some people who make large sums of money end up broke because they never learned how to manage their money—another example of our need to get back to basics.

Lotteries also cause us to want more. They now operate in 47 states and the District of Columbia, and some $50 billion is spent annually for lottery tickets.

## *What We Can Do*

### Train up a Child

If parents keep silent, advertising and the media will become our children's financial teachers. And our level of godliness is no guarantee that our children will follow in our footsteps. But by investing some prayerful guidance and love in your child's life, you can raise the next generation of faithful adults that live by God's proven principles.

Probably one of the finest generations of Israelites was the one under Joshua's command. They took the Promised Land. Then they got so busy building a life in the Promised Land that they forgot to build a future for their children.

*"All that generation also were gathered to their fathers; and there arose another generation after them who did not know the Lord, nor yet the work which He had done for Israel. Then the sons of Israel did evil in the sight of the Lord and served the Baals, and they forsook the Lord, the God of their fathers. . . . The anger of the Lord burned against Israel, and He gave them into the hands of plunderers who plundered them; and He sold them into the hands of their enemies around them, so that they could no longer stand before their enemies"* (Judges 2:10-12, 14).

In short, the Israelites began to lose the Promised Land when they didn't teach their children to follow God. Training is always the parents' responsibility.

## God's Training Method

We need to do more than teach children that the Bible is our guide and that God's principles are the ones to follow. We need to add the "why" and the "who."

God instructs us to teach children this way: *"Children, obey your parents in the Lord, for this is right. Honor your father and mother (which is the first commandment with a promise), so that it may be well with you, and that you may live long on the earth. Fathers, do not provoke your children to anger; but bring them up in the discipline and instruction of the Lord"* (Ephesians 6:1-4).

God tells children to honor and obey their parents, but He doesn't stop there. He tells them what the results will be: *"That it may be well with you, and that you may live long on the earth."*

But that's not all. We have the privilege of taking our children beyond the rule and even beyond the reason for the rule. We get to take them to the Ruler. Jesus said, *"Let the little children alone, and do not hinder them from coming to Me"* (Matthew 19:14).

We can show our children that God's ways and principles work out best for us because God is good and faithful and loves us. Talk about setting them up for life!

With each financial principle we establish not only the rule but the reason, and with the reason we help them get to know the Ruler. Then we take what is learned and apply the principles to other areas of our children's lives, using what they learned in finances as the example. Doing this will elevate your parenting to a level far above average!

## An Indicator of the Heart

Teaching children about money is a crucial part of their training, because a person's attitude toward finances is an indicator of his or her heart. Jesus said, *"For where your treasure is, there your heart will be also"* (Matthew 6:21).

Remember the rich young ruler in Luke 18? What was the one thing he lacked? Jesus told him to sell everything and give to the poor. Then he would have what he lacked: treasure in heaven. Jesus says we can get our hearts in the right place by putting our treasures in the right place.

In His teachings and parables—whether the rich young ruler,

the lost son, the widow's mite, the sheep and the goats, or many others—Jesus taught that what we do with our money and our possessions is a direct reflection of what is in our hearts. Our checkbooks are like thermometers, measuring the heat of our love and commitment to God and His principles.

Jesus emphasized that we *"cannot serve both God and wealth [money]"* (Luke 16:13). We will serve one or the other. Our heart will be devoted to the one we serve, and our actions will show it.

If we allow our children to buy into the world's way of handling finances, following whatever progressive thought is currently in vogue, they will naturally learn and apply the world's principles. And barring a transformation, they will do it for the rest of their lives.

In other words, their hearts will follow where their treasures have been buried. However, if we teach our children God's way of handling finances, they'll learn His principles and be able to govern their lives in the best possible way.

## *Some Key Lessons for Our Children*

### Stewardship

Perhaps the most important lesson in our children's financial training is the concept of stewardship, which says that money is a trust given to us by God. Therefore, it should be handled in the way the Master directs.

By teaching this concept, we lay the foundation to teach much more, such as learning what the Bible says to do with money and praying for wisdom and direction in its usage.

Once children have learned to follow God's Word and pray for wisdom and direction in their finances, it is easy to take them to the next lesson: Jesus is Lord of our entire life. He wants us to follow His principles and pray for wisdom concerning every area of our life: behavior, money, character, marriage, career, ministry, and everything else.

But suppose we don't teach our children how to handle money according to God's stewardship principle. Suppose we teach—even if only by example—that we can do anything we want with money because it's not really important to God. The effects are far-reaching. The misleading principles of "Do what seems right to you" and "Make your own decisions" become our children's foundation, a foundation of independence from God—not a good thing!

Undoubtedly, the results of godly teaching are much more desirable. When we instruct our children to follow the teaching of the Bible in their finances, we've laid the foundation for God's Word to be life's guidebook. Having built the foundation in a hands-on area like finances, it is easy then to direct them to the Bible with every question life poses.

## The Church

Another important part of our children's financial training is showing them the importance of the church. If we teach our children through instruction and example to give to the church, it gives us the opportunity to teach them their place and responsibility in the church. It also allows us to teach them about the role of the church and church community in their lives.

Teaching our children to give helps introduce them to what we call the first principle. Often our reactions (and our children's) to giving to the church, to missions, and to meeting the needs of others is, "Hey, what about my needs?"

The first principle is that God is our provider. Our incomes, savings, jobs, investments, and possessions are not our security or source of provision. They may be the means God uses to provide for us, but He is the ultimate provider and our only source of security. We are to keep our eyes on Him.

**Financial Contentment**

Have you ever noticed how people run from one thing to another in search of contentment? When the thrill of a new purchase is gone, they buy another. When the thrill of a relationship is gone, they begin another.

But true contentment is not found in "things." Peace comes from learning to trust God's control and timing. This learning to trust is both a choice and a process, one that involves the consistent, long-term application of God's principles.

The word contentment literally means "to be enough." Paul said, *"Not that I speak from want, for I have learned to be content in whatever circumstances I am. I know how to get along with humble means, and I also know how to live in prosperity; in any and every circumstance I have learned the secret of being filled and going hungry, both of having abundance and suffering need. I can do all things through Him who strengthens me"* (Philippians 4:11-13).

Paul was content even when he was in need. That's because God was his "enough." Our contentment is to spring from our relationship with God and our growing trust in Him. You can help train your emotions and attitude by praying frequently, "I love you, Lord, and you are enough."

## Honesty in Finances

Children are almost universal in presenting parents with two golden opportunities to teach honesty. First comes the temptation to tell a lie when the truth will get them into trouble. The second is when, after beginning to realize the value of money, they find some lying around the house and claim it as their own.

The first occasion is an opportunity to teach children to be honest in what they say. The second is an ideal time to begin teaching them to be honest in what they do. As parents we often leap on the first situation and are less responsive to the second one. But money innocently picked up is an ideal opportunity to teach respect for personal property and the value of money. And most importantly, we can teach that when we are always honest in what we do, we aren't under pressure to be dishonest in what we say.

We also can teach children about honesty through our own lives. Real life events are the lessons children remember best. For example, one parent drove all the way back to a store after finding that the clerk hadn't charged enough. On another occasion, a parent waited in line to give a store owner

25 cents that a vending machine had accidentally fed into a change slot. As children watch their parents do such things, they are likely to remember what they saw. And as they remember, they will also remember what their parents were trying to teach them.

## How Do We Present These Lessons?

### In Love

*"If I speak with the tongues of men and of angels, but do not have love, I have become a noisy gong or a clanging cymbal. And if I have the gift of prophecy, and know all mysteries and all knowledge; and if I have all faith, so as to remove mountains, but do not have love, I am nothing. And if I give all my possessions to feed the poor, and if I surrender my body to be burned, but do not have love, it profits me nothing"* (1 Corinthians 13:1-3).

If we could be perfect parents, as far as our performance goes, and teach our children to accomplish all the great things listed in these verses, without love it wouldn't gain us anything or make our children into anything.

A child is a "trust." We are stewards of our children for a short time, and someday, when they're ready to leave the nest, we'll realize how short that time is. Our children are precious, and so are the moments we spend with them.

Furthermore, God not only requires our children to obey and follow us as parents, He also requires that we follow Him.

We need to treat our children as if they are God's children and we are babysitting for Him. We use the word babysitting to conjure up a familiar picture. Recall the moment when the parents arrive home and the babysitter is asked, "How did it go?"

That babysitter knows that this is the moment of accountability. A positive report about the children is great. But the nervousness comes from the real underlying questions: "How did you do?" and "Did you treat my children well?"

If the thought of God coming to pick up His "children" today and asking us and them how it went is a little unnerving, we can pray and ask for His forgiveness and help. God wants the best for us and our children—that's grace parenting—and He's ready to help.

We need to treat and teach our children with respect as fellow heirs to God's kingdom and as budding young children of God.

We need to reflect a loving, forgiving, Father God in our parenting. As He is patient and kind with us, so we need to be patient and kind with our children. As He forgives and instructs, so we are to forgive and gently instruct.

At the same time, we must not misconstrue love as mere tolerance that doesn't train and discipline our children. If we don't discipline and correct them, the Bible says we don't love them. *"He who withholds his rod hates his son, but he who loves him disciplines him diligently"* (Proverbs 13:24). As you ask God for wisdom and guidance in raising your children, He will be faithful to answer your prayer and meet your needs in this area.

## Using Foundational Teaching

We explain God's principles to our children by using the ingredients for foundational teaching:

- what the Bible says,
- simple words and real life examples and allegories, and
- the reason and Ruler behind the rule.

Suppose we're teaching our children about tithing. A good example would be Abram giving a tithe to Melchizedek (Genesis 14) after winning a battle against four kings. Melchizedek was "priest of God Most High." Because it's a story, it will hold our children's interest and be easier for them to remember.

Point out that Abram took a tenth of everything he acquired in the battle and gave it back to God. By doing so, he was showing everyone that it was God who had helped him win.

Now we draw the parallel to ourselves by reading, *"Honor the Lord from your wealth and from the first of all your produce; so your barns will be filled with plenty and your vats will overflow with new wine"* (Proverbs 3:9-10).

We need to explain how the tithe reflects God's ownership of everything and His care for us, just as it did in Abram's life. Then we tell our children a real life story of how we began to tithe and some ways that God took care of us. If they are too young to understand percentages, we can take 10 dimes and physically demonstrate what we mean.

Next, take the time to explain the reason and Ruler behind the rule. Give a simple explanation of how this money helps the church pay its bills and its pastors and help needy people. We should explain that this is important to God because He loves us and the people our money is helping.

After teaching the principle of tithing, we need to help our children implement tithing practically in their own lives. We don't just tell them to do it; we walk through it with them. We show them how to separate their own money to give God His part and remind them to put it in the offering at church.

Once we've started our children tithing, we need to consistently help them with it. We need to reinforce the principles and the teaching behind the principles at regular intervals.

For example, we can pray together on the way to church. We can thank God for taking care of us and our family and for the opportunity to give to the people at church. When our children are ready and curious, we can teach them more on the topic from the Bible. We need to look and pray for the opportunities.

Also, a really important part of parenting is to watch for and identify God at work. For example, if God opens up an opportunity for our children to earn more money, or they get an incredible deal on something they have been saving for, or some money comes to them through an unexpected channel, we can point it out to our children as a way God has honored their faith and obedience and has taken care of them.

If you would like a resource to help teach your K-5th grader how to live a financially faithful life, purchase a copy of the

*FamilyTimes Stewardship Virtue Pack* available from Crown or your local bookstore. It contains stories, music, video, and discussion topics that you and your child can do together.

## Section 2: Parenting Economics 101

### Parenting Economics Rule #1

The family is a community, and everyone in the family shares in the opportunities, responsibilities, rewards, and income of that community.

In line with this thought, giving children allowances and requiring them to do household duties should not be tied together like a work-for-hire agreement.

As part of the family community, each person is responsible for certain household duties for which he or she is not paid: washing dishes, cleaning floors, cleaning bathrooms, doing the laundry, gardening, dusting, and painting. These provide everyone's needs—not just one person's. Our children should be responsible for more than cleaning up after themselves.

The Bible says, *"Do not merely look out for your own personal interests, but also for the interests of others"* (Philippians 2:4).

Family community benefits are food, shelter, clothing, relationship, and also an allowance. Since the children's allowance should not be tied to specific tasks as payment, it can be explained as follows.

- The income that is earned for the family is household and community income and is to be used for that purpose.

- As part of the family or community,

children receive an income (or allowance) until they have income of their own. One of the primary purposes for this income is to help them begin to learn how to handle finances.

## Parenting Economics Rule #2

Establish job opportunities inside and outside the home that serve as a training ground for individual work and remuneration.

If allowances are not tied to work, how can we begin to teach our children a work ethic and the idea that work equals pay? We do this by giving our children the opportunity to earn extra money doing jobs that go beyond cleaning up after themselves or fulfilling their share of family or community responsibilities.

These jobs can be posted on a "job board," which might be a 12-by-18-inch piece of cardboard with the words "Quality Labor Required" at the top.

Attach post-it notes to the board with the names of the jobs and how much they will pay. For example: clean out refrigerator—$3, clean garage—$6, wash and vacuum car—$4.

On the bottom of the job board, write the "Terms of Employment," which are as follows.

- Every job must be inspected before payment is made.

- No job partially done will receive payment.

- Pray before choosing jobs. Be sure you don't take on more than you can do.

- All jobs must be done diligently. Do them quickly, do them well, and work hard.

- All regular chores must be completed before taking a job from the job board.

- Management reserves the right not to pay for slack, slow, or sloppy work. Management also reserves the right to pay bonuses for jobs that are well done.

It's best not to pay children by the hour. It's better to pay them by the job. This helps establish money as a means of exchange. The quicker they get the job done, the more valuable their time is.

In addition, it may be a good idea to establish an age range for some jobs. For example: "Sweep the porch—$1; must be 6 to 7 and good with a broom."

Finally, when we're employing our children, we don't want to be too harsh. We always should have our children watch us do a job at least once before we ask them to do it on their own.

When they are ready, we need to be there to help and encourage them—but not nag them. We shouldn't be surprised if they work slowly and sloppily at first.

Furthermore, it's much more helpful to make the task joyful, play a bit, have some fun in the process, encourage them, and praise them when they get it right. If they do it wrong, we simply offer to show them a second time how it's done.

With each job we train our children to do, we should train them in diligence and the work ethic. We can remind them they are working for the best boss possible: God. *"Whatever you do, do your work heartily, as for the Lord rather then for men"* (Colossians 3:23).

## Parenting Economics Rule #3

Be sure allowances do not discourage joy in community involvement or encourage laziness.

We need to be careful about setting allowance amounts. Children's allowances should be enough to look forward to, enough to enable us to begin teaching them how to manage their money, but not enough that all their wants and desires are met so they have no need for extra jobs. For this reason allowances may have to be reviewed and adjusted periodically.

Ultimately, we need to wean our children off allowances and on to their own earned income. Therefore we need to be sure our raises don't keep pace, percentage-wise, with their budgets. Their allowances should become an ever-decreasing portion of their spending plans.

## Parenting Economics Rule #4

Be consistent in the teaching, training, and disciplining process.

Once we have established an allowance amount and frequency, we need to add it into our family budget and pay it as we would any other bill—consistently and on time. Also, if we establish a rule for our children, with rewards for compliance and penalties for not complying with the rule, it is essential that we always follow through.

## Parenting Economics Rule #5

Everything we do should reflect real life as closely as possible—its systems, its rewards, and its penalties.

For example, we shouldn't pay our children for a job that is half done or not done well. Rather, if they still need training, we can help them complete the job but not pay until it is finished. In the job market we don't get half pay for half a job. We get no pay, and if not remedied, we lose our jobs.

## Parenting Economics Rule #6

Take the cloaking devices off family finances. It's important to let our children know about, see the workings of, and get involved in family and household finances.

## Parenting Economics Rule #7

When assigning tasks, giving job opportunities, and deciding on training and discipline methods, take the individual child into consideration—strengths, weaknesses, abilities, and problems.

Sometimes, when we think we've run up against bad attitudes in our children, we may be dealing with misunderstood aptitudes. Some very good books have been written about children's personality types, learning methods, aptitudes, gifts, and even how their birth order affects their perceptions. One thing is for sure: Children are not born as blanks for us to program. God made each one unique.

For example, some personality types are very meticulous and detailed; they love to count and budget every penny. This type may find the idea of plan management easy but may need encouragement to actually spend some of their neatly counted money.

Another thing to consider is gender. God made males and females different. It's important to be careful not to compare our children's strengths and weaknesses. We must deal with each child as an individual and ask God for individual wisdom.

On the other hand, personality differences and uniqueness are never valid excuses for violating God's laws or principles. We are all responsible to follow God's principles.

## Section 3: Tools for Training

An effective way to ensure that you cover all of God's financial principles in your instruction is to divide them into four logical groupings:

**Group 1**—Stewardship, trusting God, tithing/giving, and generosity.

**Group 2**—Contentment, honesty, and diligence.

**Group 3**—Spending plan management and long-term financial planning.

**Group 4**—Saving/investing, spending, and credit/debt.

When teaching each of these areas, use the following tools for the practical teaching and training that need to be done.

### Family Motto

Family mottos are easy to remember. Therefore, they're not easy to forget. For example, if you're teaching children about telling the truth and keeping their word (honesty), your motto might be, "If I say it, I'll do it. If I say it, it's the truth. You can count on it!" Ground your mottos in God's Word. In fact, you may even want to use a portion of Scripture as your motto.

## Bible Story

When teaching a lesson or principle from God's Word, a story from the Bible to illustrate the lesson strengthens the concept and makes it more solid.

## Faith Story

We also advise that the Bible story be followed with a personal faith story that illustrates the lesson.

## Memory Verse

By memorizing Bible verses, children can readily refer to them when they have life decisions to make (the same is true for adults). We also need to help our children understand these verses so God's Spirit can use them as a guide when financial decisions must be made. Remember, since the purpose of a memory verse is its application, understanding it is more important than word-for-word accuracy.

## Definition

Give simple definitions of the words (stewardship, honesty, and so forth) and simple explanations of the principles these words represent, and write them in language children will understand. You can use them as an aid or simply read them to your children. Then, if needed, you can explain the concept further.

## Activities

Instead of just talking to your children, use activities to help you in the teaching and training process. These activities should be fun as well as educational.

 **Two Examples of These Tools at Work**

Examples of how to use these tools with all 12 financial teaching areas are found in the book *Financial Parenting* (Moody Publishing), by Larry Burkett and Rick Osborne.

We don't have enough space here to provide such an extensive explanation. However, to show you how these tools work, we will cover two of the 12 financial areas: stewardship and spending plan management.

Once you review these two examples, you can create your own family mottos, stories, memory verses, and so forth for each of the remaining 10 financial areas.

## *Example #1: Stewardship*

### Family Motto

"We're looking after our money, for the Master."

### Bible Story

The faithful stewards (Luke 19:12-26). We can read this parable with our children and explain that God gives us things to care for. He wants us to use them wisely, according to His principles. If God owns what we have, then we must use it the way He wants us to. God does it this way because He loves us and knows how things will work out best. When we are obedient with what He gives us, He will be able to trust us with more.

## Faith Story

Tell the children a story about a time you chose to follow God's instructions instead of your own ideas and how everything worked out.

## Memory Verse

*"The earth is the Lord's, and all it contains, the world, and those who dwell in it"* (Psalm 24:1).

## Definition

Stewardship means that God owns everything. He gives us things to take care of (to manage). Since everything belongs to God, we need to take care of it the way He tells us to in the Bible. When we do that, we can trust God to take care of us, and God can trust us with more. We should want to be the best stewards we can possibly be for God.

## Activities

Play the "It All Belongs to God" game. (Parents should play the game too.)

Take out scissors, paper, pencils, and glue, as well as old magazines and newspapers. Find one big piece of paper or cardboard and put it in the center of

the table. Have everyone draw or find pictures or words that represent everything the family owns—from the house to the children's toys. Next, glue or tape them down in a collage all over the paper or cardboard.

Also add words or representational pictures for intangible things, such as life, family, relationships, friends, salvation, talents, careers, and so on.

If your children are too old for the collage, have everyone write a list and see who can come up with the longest list in a certain time period. Doing it room by room in the house and awarding points for each room could add fun. See who the winner is when you've finished going through the house.

In the older-age version of the game, we can set aside one room as an "intangible room," where players will add intangible items to their lists. Our goal is to go beyond physical things to everything God has given us, which includes who we are as well as what we have.

Before beginning either version of the game, it's important to explain its purpose: so we can give everything back to God.

When you're finished with the collage or lists, you can pray a short prayer together, thanking God for everything He's made you stewards over (managers of). Then you can give it all back to Him and ask for His wisdom and guidance in using it.

Now, clean up the clutter and have a treat of some kind or do something the children really like to do. It's important not to belabor a teaching activity. When you've finished, emphasize the point of the activity; then give a reward of some kind.

Here are some tips for teaching the financial area of steward-ship.

1. When making a purchasing decision, we can pray a simple prayer out loud for our children to hear. First we can tell God we want to be good stewards. Then we can ask Him for wisdom and direction in our purchasing decision.

2. When our families are faced with major decisions, such as moving, buying a home, replacing a car, changing careers, or even deciding what to do with surplus income, we can pray together as families and let the children in on how God directs.

## *Example #2: Spending Plan Management*

### Family Motto

"Pray, plan, and write it out; follow it without a doubt."

### Bible Story

Gideon's plan (Judges 6-7). Read this to your children if they are older. If you have younger children, read it and retell it, or read the story to them out of a Bible storybook.

We can explain to our children that Gideon gathered a large number of men for his army. God let him know he didn't need that many to get the job done. God pared back Gideon's army to a mere 300 men; then He gave Gideon wisdom so he could defeat the massive army of his enemy with just those men—with God's help, of course.

We can let our children know that when it comes to money, we often think we need a lot—maybe even that there is no such thing as too much. But it's not how much we have that matters, it's following God's principles and asking for His wisdom. Then, as we're obedient and trust Him, He will help us win the battle—having enough. This doesn't necessarily mean God will give us more. Instead, He may help us get the most out of what we have.

### Faith Story

Tell your children a story about how you learned to manage a spending plan and the benefits it brought.

### Memory Verse

*"The LORD said to Gideon, 'I will deliver you with the 300 men who lapped and will give the Midianites into your hands; so let all the other people go, each man to his home'"* (Judges 7:7).

### Definition

We manage money when we write down a plan for what we are going to do with our money.

The first step in a Christian's spending plan should be to figure the amount of the tithe. Other items in the plan include taxes, bills and expenses, spending money, and savings. The two basic steps to a spending plan are exactly what our motto says.

1. Pray, plan, and write down the plan.

2. Follow the plan.

## Activities

As soon as children are old enough to understand what money is and to receive and spend it, they are ready for a "pre-plan." The idea is to take them gradually from a pre-plan to a full 15-category budget by the time they live on their own. We will suggest at least two other stages between pre-plan and a full-blown spending plan, but it's important to expand, contract, or alter these to fit our own children's expenditures.

## Pre-Plan (ages 3-8)

The *ABC Learning Bank* (available on Crown's Web site or by calling 800-722-1976), is the perfect tool for the pre-plan. It is divided into three connected storage sections representing giving, saving, and spending. You may also choose to use three jars or envelopes labeled "giving," "saving," and "spending."

Three-, four- and five-year-olds should be given three coins (or three bills) and instructed to put one in each container.

Around six or seven years of age, children should be given percentages. Ten percent of their money goes to tithing, 50 percent to savings, and 40 percent to spending. We will have to help them in this process at first.

Also, we need to be sure our children are given their money so they can divide it easily. For example, $10 could easily be divided into $1 (10 percent for giving), $5 (50 percent for saving) and $4 (40 percent for spending).

The distribution of money should be as follows:

- "dump and give,"

- "dip and spend," and

- "want and save."

"Dump and give" happens on Sunday morning when we help our children dump their money out of the giving compartment and give it to the church.

"Dip and spend" happens when money is needed. "Want and save" stays in the bank for now.

At this level, the only thing that should be written down is the savings, or "want and save" goal. This saving goal should be an object inexpensive enough that children won't feel like they have to save forever to get it. Remember that to a very young child, a month may seem like an eternity. The object needs to be more expensive and special than what they can get with their "dip and spend" money, and the required saving time should be increased as they are ready to handle it.

Write whatever your children are saving for on post-it notes and attach them to the bank (or jar or envelope). You may also want to attach pictures of the items to the bank.

We want to help our children stick to this goal; it's their first experience with making and following a spending plan.

### Mini-Plan (ages 9-12)

A "mini-plan" can still be housed in the *ABC Learning Bank*, but a little more budgeting or writing is now required. It will be necessary to get a small notebook to go along with the bank. The notebook is the start of our children's training to use a bank book and spending plan ledger.

An important lesson for this age group involves restraint. Just because the container has a certain amount of money in it, children cannot necessarily spend it all on one thing. That money has different purposes according to the plan, which at this point will consist of four categories:

- giving (10 percent);
- saving-a-little (25 percent for short-term savings);
- saving-a-lot (25 percent for long-term savings); and
- spending (40 percent).

The two categories of "saving-a-little" and "saving-a-lot" re-place the "want and save" category of the pre-plan but are still kept in the same saving section of the bank.

We suggest that children's notebooks be kept as follows.

**Page 1**—Write the four mini-plan categories with their per-centages.

**Page 2**—On the top of the page write the spending plan motto.

1. Pray, plan, and write it out.

2. Follow it without a doubt.

The bottom of Page 2 is reserved for "Saving-a-little," which is a short-term goal. (Not all savings should be allocated be-fore it's saved, but right now we are trying to teach them to save and plan for what they want and desire. The rest will come later.)

In the middle of Page 2, put a photo (optional) of the short-term item children are saving for.

Have the children think of something they want that will take three to six weeks to save for (help them figure this out). Have them write down what they decide on and what it will cost. If they don't know what it will cost, the next step is to help them find out.

**Page 3**—Use this page for the Saving-a-little Diary. Each time children put money into their savings bank, they should write on this page how much they've put toward their goal.

**Page 4**—At the top of this page, rewrite the motto. In the middle, put a photo of the long-term savings goal.

The bottom of Page 4 is reserved for Saving-a-lot. Children should have a goal that will take three to six months to reach. They should write how much that goal will cost. (After our children save successfully a few times, and as they get older, we can allow them to save for things that will take longer.)

**Page 5**—Use this page for the Saving-a-lot Diary. Each time children put money into their savings bank for this goal, they should write the amount.

In the beginning, make sure that savings goals won't take too long. Children should be able to reach their goals quickly so they can become excited about the process.

When they reach their goals we can become excited with them. It will be helpful to praise them for saving and go through the spending procedure with them right away.

If we delay the purchase—the gratification and pay-off for all their hard work—they might lose some of the motivation toward saving that we're trying to build in them.

In the mini-budget, giving should still be "dump and give" and spending should still be "dip and spend." We can let them spend this money however they wish (in keeping with family dietary and media content rules, of course).

Remember, when the spending money is gone, it's gone. We don't supplement it in any of these budgets. That would defeat the purpose. We are training our children to physically understand the value of their money as they budget it. Bailing them out gives the wrong message.

### Teen-Budget (age 13 until just before they leave the nest)

We suggest adding two other budget categories to the teen budget to help better prepare children for all-out budgeting.

1. Giving (10 percent).

2. Community "taxes" (5 percent).

3. Short-term savings (25 percent).

4. Long-term savings (25 percent).

5. Expenses (10 percent).

6. Spending (25 percent).

It's time to take your children to the bank and have them talk to the teller and open a savings account and a checking account. Be sure they ask all the right questions and the teller adequately explains how things work.

Perhaps you wonder, "Why two accounts? Starting with two accounts continues the consistent message: It's not all one spending source.

Teach your teenagers how to reconcile their bank statements and how to keep their check registers. Also, make any and all payments due to them by check for allowances and job board earnings. This will remove the temptation to spend cash before it's in the bank.

**Family Tax?**

Before going any further, let's deal with the two added categories in the teen budget. The first of these is community "taxes."

The saying goes, "There are two things in life that are certain: death and taxes." If our teenagers know Jesus, we've prepared them for the biggest of the two. Now it's time to prepare them for taxes.

Jesus said, *"Render to Caesar the things that are Caesar's; and to God the things that are God's"* (Matthew 22:21). We can read the story surrounding this verse with our teenagers when they add this category to their budgets.

We should explain that taxes are for community betterment through community contribution. We can point out the good, practical things around us we take for granted that are paid for by taxes. Remember that our negative economic circumstances are not simply the result of taxation; they result from the abuses of debt financing and government handouts.

So, what do we do with the money? One thing we can do is establish a community tax box. We should contribute to it ourselves, perhaps matching what our teenagers put into it. Later we can decide as a family how this money is to be spent.

It should be spent on something that mutually benefits the whole family. It could be a long-term goal, like a barbecue grill or a computer. Or it could be a more immediate goal, like buying a new video for the family each month.

## Expenses

The other added category in the teen budget is expenses. Perhaps the largest budget category in adult life is regular bills and expenses. We suggest that teenagers be introduced to this category, starting with 10 percent of their income.

We can figure what approximately 10 percent of their total income is. Next, help them find an expense that needs to be paid on a regular basis that is close to that amount.

This expense could be lessons of some sort (gymnastics, dance, voice); monthly dues at the community center; a telephone of their own (billed directly to them); or several less expensive items, such as a Christian magazine subscription or the extra cost of call-waiting on the family phone (so they can talk to their friends without affecting everyone else). The key is to match the expenses with each of our children by finding things they are interested in.

When our teenagers start getting their bills, we should work with them to make sure they get into the habit of keeping their paperwork in order and paying their bills on time.

We should have them find a special place, such as a desk drawer, for their financial paperwork. We need to make sure they keep everything—checkbook, savings book, bank statements, receipts, bills, their spending plan book, and so forth—in this one place.

**NOTE:** The expense category should not go to the payment of a debt as a result of buying something over time with payments. That would invert the save-then-spend policy we are trying to teach our teenagers and put them on the world's track of buying before paying.

Teenagers will need to keep spending plan books, and we'll need to help them set up those books. (Loose-leaf binders with pockets are a good idea.) The books should be arranged as follows.

**Page 1**—Write the spending plan two-step motto.

1. Pray, plan, and write it out.

2. Follow it without a doubt.

**Page 2**—Write the six spending plan categories and their percentages.

**Page 3**—Establish a giving record and keep track of each gift (amount and date). When teenagers first move away from dump-and-give, it's easy for them to forget whether or not they gave in a particular month.

This page should also record extra giving, helping others, helping the needy, or special offerings. Teenagers can list family "faith projects" here too.

At this stage of plan management (budgeting), extra giving

should first come out of spending. This will help demonstrate the immediate sacrifice needed to follow God and give.

If the giving goal is greater, we should help teenagers adjust their short-term savings goals. Or they could even make meeting a certain need one of their short-term savings goals.

**Page 4**—Write what the family has decided to spend the community tax money on and keep a record of payments made. These payments should be made in cash so there won't be an extra accounting burden for the family administrator.

**Page 5**—Short-term savings. This is the same as in the mini-plan, except with an average three- to six-month goal.

**Page 6**—Long-term savings. Teenagers should have a "financial plan," and they should begin to line up this category with that plan.

For example, suppose a teenage daughter has prayed and established a plan to attend a university. If she needs to save to meet that goal, then her long-term savings should go in that direction now.

If she wants to buy a computer, and it's not part of her long-term plan, then it is a desire. She'll need to contribute to her short-term savings for a longer time in order to get it.

Have teenagers put a copy of their long-term savings plans into their spending plan books right beside their long-term savings. This will allow them to track the two together.

**Page 7**—Expenses. Have teenagers keep a record of the dates and accounts of their payments. These should be made by check. The payment contract or paperwork and each month's invoice or bill can be kept in the pocket of the binder.

**Page 8** (and the rest of the book)—A general "What did I make and where did it go?" page should be done for each month. Their money-in should balance their money-out or money-allocated.

All of this might be simple for some teenagers and extremely difficult for others. We will need to determine the right age for them to move to the teen budget.

It would be better for them to be consistent on the mini-plan for a longer time than to start them on a system on which they will fail. You don't want them to be discouraged.

Once they start, it is crucial that you don't demand and abandon! Work with them as long as it takes for them to get it. You want to do it with them—not for them. They'll tell us if we stay too long; independence will speak after confidence is instilled.

## Moving to a Full Budget

When our children are about ready to leave the nest, we need to help them make the transition to a full budget. For example, the spending plan used by Crown Financial Ministries consists of 15 categories: tithe, housing, automobile, debts, clothing, medical expenses, school/child care, taxes, food, insurance, entertainment/recreation, savings, miscellaneous, investments, and nonallocated surplus.

At this point, if we haven't already done it, it is important to bring our children in on our family spending plan and into the process of managing it. We can show them how much we spend on Housing, Automobile, Food, Clothes, and the rest.

We also can let our children manage our family finances for six months under our supervision. This is very much like a teenager learning to drive. No one simply hands over the car keys to a 16-year-old and says, "Good luck! See you later." Instead, hours are spent training teenagers so they can get the feel of being behind the wheel.

In addition, when children reach the level of handling their spending plans without difficulty, we can add other planning elements to their lives. We can buy them day planners and help them keep their basic life schedules and devotional diaries. We want to train them to manage not only their money but their time and energy. The skill of managing a spending plan can be applied to every area of life.

For information on additional resources that teach these concepts, check out the following studies that can be done at home, church, or in some schools as additional study:

- *The ABC's of Handling Money God's Way* by Howard and Bev Dayton (for ages 5-7)

- *The Secret of Handling Money God's Way* by Howard and Bev Dayton (for ages 8-12)

- *Discovering God's Way of Handling Money Teen Study* by Howard and Bev Dayton (for ages 13-17)

- *The Biblical Financial Study – Collegiate Edition* (for ages 18 and up)

- *The Biblical Financial Study – 10 Week Adult Edition* (for ages 18 and up)

## Credit Cards

We recommend that parents allow teen-agers to get a credit card and teach them how to use credit properly. At the earliest, this should happen after they have been using the teen spending plan for some time and are handling all the elements well.

Most importantly, establish some rules before going ahead with this. If parents and teenagers agree on the rules ahead of time—even to the point of writing them down—then teenagers will understand when parents enforce those rules.

When it comes to credit cards for teens, the rules are as follows.

1. Use the credit card only for spending plan items.
2. Pay it off at the end of every month.
3. Cut it up the first time it's not paid off on time.

We need to emphasize to our teenagers that debt is spending money we don't have. When we put money in the bank to save for something, we earn interest on that money. But credit works in reverse by charging us interest for borrowing the money.

When we save with a plan to purchase, we can continue to submit the plan to God's guidance. But when we "buy now, pay later," we risk running ahead of Him by committing money we haven't earned or saved yet. Or, more importantly, committing money He hasn't given us yet.

We can't be good stewards when we're running ahead of

the Master. God's plan is for us to mature, and part of maturing is developing the ability to delay gratification. In a culture that constantly promotes violating this principle, it is vital that we help our teens learn—through our example as well as our teaching—to wait until they have saved the money for something before they buy it.

**Conclusion**

Statistics show that 85 percent of people who accept Jesus as Savior do so before the age of 18. And it is estimated that over 50 percent of the world's population is now under the age of 18.

We as Christian parents and leaders need to prepare for the harvest because it truly is plentiful. We need to work with our children and prepare them as leaders for the next generation. If their lives are grounded in biblical truths, they won't be carried away like their peers. They will be ready to reap the harvest. As you take the steps to love, teach, and train your children in financial faithfulness, God will provide you with whatever you need to accomplish those goals. He is more than faithful as you trust Him.

### *A New Take on Money*
### The Alba Kids

When Tim Alba finished Crown's adult life group study, he wasn't content to just sit on the principles he'd learned. He not only shared those principles with other adults but also with his own children. Tim recognized an important truth: Stewardship begins in the home. It's the place where we have the greatest opportunity to influence the next generation—to *"train up a child in the way he should go"* (Proverbs 22:6).

Tim saw the life-changing power of God's financial principles, and in a society where so many people are looking for happiness, he witnessed one of the most awesome effects of those principles: contentment. So, he and his wife, Anna, decided to begin a family Bible study based on Crown's materials for teens and children.

They gave their 10-year-old son, Caleb, a copy of *The Secret of Handling Money God's Way*, Crown's study for older children. They gave Leslie, age 15, and Joshua, age 13, copies of Crown's teen study, *Discovering God's Way of Handling Money*.

When the children completed the studies, Tim asked each of them to write a letter to God, telling Him what they had learned.

Not long after that, during a church dinner, Tim was asked to share some inspirational words. He read the letter that his youngest son Caleb had written, and it received a tremendous response.

"The material taught in the study really grabbed Caleb," Tim says. "For one thing, he realized God had called him to do his best in his homework. Financial principles are not just about being faithful in finances but in all things. And, rather than money being something that keeps us from the Lord, it's something that can draw us to Him."

A few weeks into the study, all three children became very involved in the learning process. "It became fun," Tim says. "It was about them and the Lord, not about Dad trying to be cheap. They could have gone into the studies kicking and screaming or with quiet resistance. But it wasn't a stretch for them to participate."

Still, Tim was surprised to see them giving the same answers to questions as those given by adults in the studies he had led at church. "This helped me to see that God's financial principles are something anyone can grasp," he says.

Caleb says that before learning the principles, he really wasn't sure how to spend the money he received. Like many children, he spent freely, and in a short period of time he would grow tired of the things he had bought.

Today, all three children are more careful spenders, and they are saving and giving as well. For example, 10 percent of their money goes to the church and 5 percent goes to ministry. They put 50 percent toward their family vacation, and the other 35 percent goes for whatever they choose.

This is amazing in light of a question Tim answered during a Crown study two years ago. The question was, "What do you want from Crown?" Tim's answer was that he wanted to help children, including his own, develop a biblical perspective on money.

Now, in addition to the change he's seen in Caleb, his daughter Leslie is less affected by all the pressure to buy what everyone else is buying. His older son, Joshua, realizes that the biblical financial principles his dad emphasizes are from God; they're not just his dad's opinion.

"The beauty of the principles is that once you understand them, they're not hard to remember," says Tim, who's actively involved with Crown in his church and with the ministry's city team in Dallas. "The principles become a part of who you are. This is what I wanted for my children. I wanted them to do what was right when no one was watching, and this is especially true for that day when they leave home to go to college and live on their own."

Tim is a corporate controller for Cici's Pizza. He knows the wisdom of handling money wisely, but Crown helped to personalize this wisdom for him, and now it has done the same for his children.

"What has happened in our family is amazing, but it's not because we're anything special," he says. "We're just some average old 'bears' who happen to live in Texas. But when we stand before the Lord, we'll have something worthwhile to give Him because we followed His financial principles. I hope many other families will do the same thing. If they will, it can draw them together in ways they would not have imagined."

*"We will not hide them from their children; we will tell the next generation the praiseworthy deeds of the Lord, his power, and the wonders he has done"* (Psalm 78:4, NIV). ∎

## Your Response

### Action Steps _____

_____

_____

_____

_____

_____

_____

_____

_____

_____


### Celebration Plan _____

_____

_____

_____

_____

_____

_____

_____

# CHAPTER 3

# WRAPPING IT UP WITH HOPE

## A Divine Pattern

We began this book by emphasizing the importance of marriage and family as evidenced by God's first command to those He created in His own image. Millennia later, anthropologists still acknowledge the central role of families in every culture. God's design, while highly practical, is also highly spiritual, a reflection of the mystery of the relationship between "Christ and the church" (see Ephesians 5:32).

Pausing to meditate on the supreme importance to God of the relationship between Christ and the church—and what it cost Him to establish it—gives us a clue to His definition of commitment. Rather than laying a heavy burden on us, it should inspire us to recognize the lengths to which He will go to help us "become one flesh" (see Ephesians 5:31) physically, emotionally and spiritually.

When relationships at home are healthy, they pay huge dividends in terms of fulfillment. They help us retain significant emotional reserves to cope with other parts of life that may be troublesome.

The inverse is also true. When relationships at home are rocky, we have trouble keeping the tension out of other relationships and responsibilities. Fortunately, the home front requires only one kind of magic to remain strong: the magic of love applied consistently.

## Love Bank Accounts

Have you thought about what it means to "apply" love? Willard Harley, in his excellent book titled *Fall in Love, Stay in Love*,[1] uses an appropriate metaphor for all of us familiar with bank accounts. He speaks of making deposits in the Love Bank—very specific deposits that are the most meaningful to our partner.

He says we each have a unique set of emotional needs that, whether we are conscious of them or not, govern our feelings of love. People who don't fulfill our emotional needs tend to leave us cold. We may not actively dislike them, but we feel no warmth toward them.

However, when someone fulfills our most important emotional needs, we experience a sense of euphoria, which easily leads to the feeling of love.

This is obviously a double-edged sword, because if our most important emotional needs happen to be met—even inadvertently—by someone other than our spouse, we risk misplacing our affection.

When spouses meet these needs for each other, however, the feelings of love remain high, making it much easier to support each other through difficult times.

## Emotional Need Ratings

Consider Harley's top-ten list of emotional-need categories, and rank them in importance for you.

- Admiration
- Affection
- Conversation
- Domestic support
- Family commitment
- Financial support
- Honesty and openness
- Physical attractiveness
- Recreational companionship
- Sexual fulfillment

How you rank these is likely to differ significantly from your spouse's ranking. This difference can easily lead you to believe you are making meaningful deposits into your spouse's Love Bank because those same deposits in your Love Bank would fill it. But if your deposits don't line up with your spouse's most important emotional needs, they will fall far short of having the same effect.

Discuss these with each other, and explore the most effective ways to fill your Love Bank accounts to overflowing. You don't have to settle for a marriage that stays together through sheer force of will and grudging commitment. You can fall in love again. And again. And again.

### Investment + Time = Major Rewards

Marriage and parenting both require huge investments of time and energy. If the payoffs were immediate, great marriages and well-adjusted children would be the norm.

Unfortunately, the tedium of everyday life often distracts our attention from the account levels, presenting us with occasional bounced checks. But when we develop the right habits and make the right investments, the payoffs are beyond imagination.

Graduating to grandparenthood can be like heaven on earth. Much of it depends on the kinds of deposits you make during the decades preceding it:

- deposits that meet your spouse's most important emotional needs, and

- deposits that meet your children's most important emotional needs, including loving discipline and training.

The great thing about these kinds of deposits—and love in general—is that God has designed us for success. We don't have to be brilliant, educated, or even above average. When we choose to love as God loves, He provides the insight we need and makes up for our incomplete information. That is part of what Peter meant when he said *"love covers a multitude of sins"* (1 Peter 4:8).

### Never Too Late to Start

All of us would improve the quality of our past deposits if we could. The encouraging truth is that we can improve what we do today. And tomorrow. And the next day. And our expression of God's kind of caring, unselfish love will make all the difference.

**ENDNOTE**

1. Willard Harley, *Fall in Love, Stay in Love*. Grand Rapids: Fleming H. Revell, 2001.

## *Your Response*

### *Action Steps* _____

_____

_____

_____

_____

_____

_____

_____

_____

_____


### *Celebration Plan* _____

_____

_____

_____

_____

_____

_____

_____

# INTRODUCTION TO CHRIST

As important as our financial welfare is, it is not our highest priority. The single most important need of every person everywhere is to know God and experience the gift of His forgiveness and peace.

These five biblical truths will show you God's open door through a personal relationship with Jesus Christ.

## 1. God loves you and wants you to know Him and experience a meaningful life.

God created people in His own image, and He desires a close relationship with each of us. *"For God so loved the world, that He gave His only begotten Son, that whoever believes in Him shall not perish, but have eternal life"* (John 3:16). *"I [Jesus] came that they might have life, and have it abundantly"* (John 10:10).

God the Father loved you so much that He gave His only Son, Jesus Christ, to die for you.

## 2. Unfortunately, we are separated from God.

Because God is holy and perfect, no sin can abide in His presence. Every person has sinned, and the consequence of sin is separation from God. *"All have sinned and fall short of the glory of God"* (Romans 3:23). *"Your sins have cut you off from God"* (Isaiah 59:2, TLB).

## 3. God's only provision to bridge this gap is Jesus Christ.

Jesus Christ died on the cross to pay the penalty for our sin, bridging the gap between God and us. Jesus said, *"I am the way, and the truth, and the life; no one comes to the Father but through Me"* (John 14:6). *"God demonstrates His own love towards us, in that while we were yet sinners, Christ died for us"* (Romans 5:8).

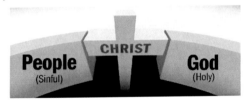

## 4. This relationship is a gift from God.

Our efforts can never achieve the perfection God requires. The only solution was to provide it to us as a gift.

When Jesus bore our sins on the cross, paying our penalty forever, He exchanged His righteousness for our guilt. By faith, we receive the gift we could never deserve.

Is that fair? Of course not! God's love exceeds His justice, resulting in mercy and grace toward us.

*"It is by grace you have been saved, through faith—and this is not from yourselves, it is the gift of God—not by works, so that no one can boast"* (Ephesians 2:8-9, NIV).

### 5. We must each receive Jesus Christ individually.

Someone has said that God has no grandchildren. Each of us is responsible before God for our own sin. We can continue to bear the responsibility and pay the consequences or we can receive the gift of Jesus' righteousness, enabling God to declare us "Not guilty!"

If you desire to know the Lord and are not certain whether you have this relationship, we encourage you to receive Christ right now. Pray a prayer similar to this suggested one:

*"God, I need You. I invite Jesus to come into my life as my Savior and Lord and to make me the person You want me to be. Thank You for forgiving my sins and for giving me the gift of eternal life."*

You may be successful in avoiding financial quicksand—and we pray you will be—but without a relationship with Christ, it won't have lasting value. Eternal perspective begins with Him.

If you ask Christ into your life, please tell some people you know who are also following Christ. They will encourage you and help you get involved in a Bible-teaching church where you can grow spiritually. And please let us know as well. We would love to help in any way we can.

# GOD'S OWNERSHIP & FINANCIAL FAITHFULNESS

How we view God determines how we live. Viewing Him as Savior is a good beginning, but growth comes when we view Him as Lord.

After losing his children and all his possessions, Job continued to worship God because he knew God was the Lord of those possessions and retained the ultimate rights over them. Realizing that God owed him nothing and he owed God everything enabled him to submit to God's authority and find contentment.

Moses walked away from his earthly inheritance, regarding *"disgrace for the sake of Christ as of greater value than the treasures of Egypt"* because he had his eye on God's reward (Hebrews 11:26, NIV).

Our willingness, like theirs, to give up a lesser value for a greater one, requires recognizing what most of the world does not: God is not only the Creator and Owner of all but also the ultimate definer of value. Those responsibilities belong to Him. He has retained them because He alone is capable of handling them.

Most of the frustration we experience in handling money comes when we take God's responsibilities on our own shoulders. Successful money management requires us to understand three aspects of God's Lordship—three roles for which He retains responsibility.

### 1. GOD OWNS IT ALL.

God owns all our possessions. *"To the Lord your God belong . . . the earth and everything in it"* (Deuteronomy 10:14, NIV). *"The earth is the Lord's, and all it contains"* (Psalm 24:1).

Leviticus 25:23 identifies Him as the owner of all the land: *"The land . . . shall not be sold permanently, for the land is Mine."* Haggai 2:8 says that He owns the precious metals: *"'The silver is Mine and the gold is Mine,' declares the Lord of hosts."*

Even our body—the one thing for which we would tend to claim total ownership—is not our own. *"Or do you not know that your body is a temple of the Holy Spirit who is in you, whom you have from God, and that you are not your own?"* (1 Corinthians 6:19).

The Lord created all things, and He never transferred the ownership of His creation to people. In Colossians 1:17 we are told that, *"In Him all things hold together."* At this very moment the Lord holds everything together by His power. As we will see throughout this study, recognizing God's ownership is crucial in allowing Jesus Christ to become the Lord of our money and possessions.

## • Yielding Our Ownership to His Lordship

If we are to be genuine followers of Christ, we must transfer ownership of our possessions to Him. *"None of you can be My disciple who does not give up all his own possessions"* (Luke 14:33). Sometimes He tests us by asking us to give up the very possessions that are most important to us.

The most vivid example of this in Scripture is when God instructed Abraham, *"Take now your son, your only son, whom you love, Isaac . . . and offer him there as a burnt offering"* (Genesis 22:2). When Abraham obeyed, demonstrating his willingness to give up his most valuable possession, God responded, *"Do not lay a hand on the boy . . . now I know that you fear God, because you have not withheld from Me your son"* (Genesis 22:12, NIV).

When we acknowledge God's ownership, every spending decision becomes a spiritual decision. No longer do we ask, "Lord, what do You want me to do with my money?" It becomes, "Lord, what do You want me to do with Your money?" When we have this attitude and handle His money according to His wishes, spending and saving decisions become as spiritual as giving decisions.

## • Recognizing God's Ownership

Our culture—the media, even the law—says that what you possess, you own. Acknowledging God's ownership requires a transformation of thinking, and this can be difficult. Many people say that God owns it all while they cling desperately to possessions that they think define them.

Here are a number of practical suggestions to help us recognize God's ownership.

- For the next 30 days, meditate on 1 Chronicles 29:11-12 when you first awake and just before going to sleep.

- For the next 30 days, ask God to make you aware of His ownership and help you to be thankful for it.

- Establish the habit of acknowledging God's ownership every time you buy something.

Recognizing God's ownership is important in learning contentment. When you believe you own something, you are more vulnerable to its circumstances. If it suffers loss or damage, your attitude can swing quickly from happy to discontented.

Recognizing it as God's loss doesn't make it irrelevant, but it does change your perspective. Now you can focus on how He will use this incident in causing *"all things to work together for good to those who love God, to those who are called according to His purpose"* (Romans 8:28).

## 2. GOD CONTROLS IT ALL.

Besides being Creator and Owner, God is ultimately in control of every event that occurs upon the earth. *"We adore* you as being in control of every-thing" (1 Chronicles 29:11, TLB). *"Whatever the Lord pleases, He does, in heaven and in earth"* (Psalm 135:6). And in the book of Daniel, King Nebuchadnezzar stated: *"I praised the Most High; I honored and glorified him who lives forever. . . . He does as he pleases with the powers of heaven and the peoples of the earth. No one can hold back his hand or say to him: 'What have you done?'"* (Daniel 4:34-35, NIV).

God is also in control of difficult events. *"I am the Lord, and there is no other, the One forming light and creating darkness, causing well-being and creating calamity; I am the Lord who does all these"* (Isaiah 45:6-7).

It is important for us to realize that our heavenly Father uses even seemingly devastating circumstances for ultimate good in the lives of the godly. *"We know that God causes all things to work together for good to those who love God, to those who are called according to His purpose"* (Romans 8:28). God allows difficult circumstances for three reasons.

## • He accomplishes His intentions.

This is illustrated in the life of Joseph, who was sold into slavery as a teenager by his jealous brothers. Joseph later said to his brothers: *"Do not be distressed and do not be angry with yourselves for selling me here, because it was to save lives that God sent me ahead of you. . . . It was not you who sent me here, but God. . . . You intended to harm me, but God*

*intended it for good to accomplish what is now be-*
*ing done, the saving of many lives"* (Genesis 45:5, 8;
50:20, NIV).

### • He develops our character.

Godly character, something that is precious in His
sight, is often developed during trying times. *"We also
rejoice in our sufferings, because we know that suffering produces perseverance; perseverance, character"*
(Romans 5:3-4, NIV).

### • He disciplines His children.

*"Those whom the Lord loves He disciplines. . . . He
disciplines us for our good, so that we may share His
holiness. All discipline for the moment seems not to
be joyful, but sorrowful; yet to those who have been
trained by it, afterwards it yields the peaceful fruit of
righteousness"* (Hebrews 12:6,10-11).

When we are disobedient, we can expect our loving
Lord to discipline us, often through difficult circumstances. His purpose is to encourage us to abandon
our sin and to "share His holiness."

You can be at peace knowing that your loving heavenly
Father is in control of every situation you will ever face.
He will use every one of them for a good purpose.

### 3. GOD PROVIDES IT ALL.

God promises to provide our needs. *"But
seek first His kingdom and His righteousness, and all these things [food and*

*clothing] will be added to you"*
(Matthew 6:33).

The same God who fed manna to the children of Israel during their 40 years of wandering in the wilderness and who fed 5,000 with only five loaves and two fish has promised to provide our needs. This is the same God who told Elijah, *"I have commanded the ravens to provide for you there. . . . The ravens brought him bread and meat in the morning and bread and meat in the evening"* (1 Kings 17:4, 6).

## God—Both Predictable and Unpredictable

God is totally predictable in His faithfulness to provide for our needs. What we cannot predict is how He will provide. He uses various and often surprising means—an increase in income or a gift. He may provide an opportunity to stretch limited resources through money-saving purchases. Regardless of how He chooses to provide for our needs, He is completely reliable.

Our culture believes that God plays no part in financial matters; they assume that His invisibility means He is uninvolved. They try to shoulder responsibilities that God never intended for them—burdens of ownership, control, and provision that only He can carry.

Jesus said, *"Come to Me, all who are weary and heavy-laden, and I will give you rest. Take My yoke upon you. . . . For My yoke is easy, and My burden is light"* (Matthew 11:28-30). This is the only way we can rest and enjoy the peace of God.

When we trust God to do His part in our finances, we can focus on doing our part: being financially faithful with every resource He has given us.

## Defining Financial Faithfulness

Faithfully living by God's financial principles doesn't necessarily mean having a pile of money in the bank, but it does bring an end to overdue bills and their related stress. And that's not the most important part; that's just relief from symptoms.

Consider some of the big-picture benefits:

- Assurance that God is in control of our circumstances
- Absolute faith in His promise to meet all of our needs
- A clear conscience before God
- A clear conscience with others

This is not to say that we will live on financial autopilot with no more challenges for the rest of our lives. God promises no such thing. In fact, without challenges our faith has no opportunity to be perfected or even to grow; without challenges it isn't active or visible. But peace in the midst of challenges is a miraculous quality of life, and that's what God promises when we learn to trust and follow Him fully.

With God in control, we have nothing to fear. He is the Master of the universe. His wisdom is superior to ours in every way, and no situation is too complex or hopeless for Him to solve.

God has even provided a solution for our ongoing frailties and failings. As part of His great redemption, He offers continuing forgiveness and cleansing from all unrighteousness (1 John 1:9). We make mistakes—sometimes willfully violating His plan for us—but He welcomes our confession and honors it by restoring our fellowship and renewing our guidance.

Once we begin to experience the rewards of financial faithfulness, we never want to be without them. Our deepening trust in *God's* faithfulness intensifies our desire to stay within His will, resulting in perfect peace.

Many people have inherited or achieved financial independence: a level of wealth that requires no further work or income. But apart from Christ, they don't have freedom from anxiety; they have merely replaced one set of worries with another. They often fear:

- Loss of what they have accumulated

- Loss of meaningful relationships—fearing that others only care about what they have rather than who they are

- Loss of safety as their wealth makes them a target for theft or kidnapping

- Loss of grace from others, who jealously hold them to a higher standard because of their wealth

Being financially free, on the other hand, includes freedom from these fears as well as from the oppression of envy, covetousness, and greed.

Financial faithfulness is transformation—a process that requires God's power and our participation. It is synonymous with our definition of true financial faithfulness in the *Crown Money Map™*:

1. Knowing that God owns it all.

2. Finding contentment with what He provides.

3. Being free to be all He made you to be.

This is the big picture, the framework within which wealth and material possessions take their rightful place—not as ends but as means—in God's hands.

## *Steps to Cultivate Financial Faithfulness*

Now it is time to outline the path. Since we're talking about transformation, you'll notice that some of our steps go well beyond mere money-management techniques.

### 1. TRANSFER OWNERSHIP.

Transferring ownership of every possession to God means acknowledging that He already owns them and that we will begin treating them accordingly. This includes more than just material possessions; it includes money, time, family, education, even earning potential for the future. This is essential to experience the Spirit-filled life in the area of finances (see Psalm 8:4-6).

There is no substitute for this step. If we believe we are the owners of even a single possession, then the events affecting that possession are going to affect our attitudes. God will not input His perfect will into our lives unless we first surrender our wills to Him.

However, if we make a total transfer of everything to God, He will demonstrate His ability. It is important to understand and accept God's conditions for His control (see Deuteronomy 5:32-33). God will keep His promise to provide our every need according to His perfect plan.

It is easy to say we will make a total transfer of everything to God, but it's not so easy to do. Our desire for control and our habit of self-management cause difficulty in consistently seeking God's will in the area of material things. But without a deep conviction that He is in control, we can never experience true financial faithfulness.

What a great relief it is to turn our burdens over to Him. Then, if something happens to the car, we can say, "Father, I gave this car to You; I've maintained it to the best of my ability, but I don't own it. It belongs to You, so do with it whatever You like." Then look for the blessing God has in store as a result of this attitude.

## 2. BECOME DEBT FREE.

God wants us to be free to serve Him without restriction. *"You were bought with a price; do not become slaves of men"* (1 Corinthians 7:23). *"The rich rules over the poor, and the borrower becomes the lender's slave"* (Proverbs 22:7).

Read *Debt and Bankruptcy*, another book in the *MoneyLife™ Basics Series*, for further information on this, including definitions and steps for getting out of debt. For most, this will involve sacrifice—at least initially—but the payoff is well worth it.

### 3. GIVE REGULARLY AND GENEROUSLY.

Every follower of Christ should establish tithing (10 percent of income) as a beginning point of giving and as a testimony to God's ownership. We can't say we have given total ownership to God if our actions don't back the claim.

It is through sharing that we bring His power in finances into focus. In every case, God wants us to give the first part to Him, but He also wants us to pay our creditors. This requires establishing a plan, and it will probably mean making sacrifices of wants and desires until all obligations are current.

We cannot sacrifice God's part—that is not our prerogative as faithful, obedient followers of Christ. Malachi 3:8-9 has strong words for those who "rob God." But then verses 10-12 describe His great blessing for those who tithe fully.

God, as the first giver, wants us to be like Him, and His economy rewards our generosity. *"Now this I say, he who sows sparingly will also reap sparingly, and he who sows bountifully will also reap bountifully"* (2 Corinthians 9:6).

Steps two and three combine to form an important conclusion. If, while en route to financial faithfulness, sacrifice becomes necessary—and it almost always does—our sacrifice must not come from God's or our creditor's share. We must choose areas within our other discretionary expenses to sacrifice. Consider it an opportunity to exercise faith in God's reward for our obedience.

### 4. ACCEPT GOD'S PROVISION.

To obtain financial peace, recognize and accept that God's provision is used to direct each of our lives. Often Christians lose sight of the fact that God's will can be accomplished through a withholding of funds; we think that He can direct us only by an abundance of money. But God does not choose for everyone to live in great abundance. This does not imply poverty, but it may mean that God wants us to be more responsive to His day-by-day control.

Followers of Christ must learn to live on what God provides and not give in to a driving desire for wealth or the pressure brought on by comparison with others. This necessitates planning our lifestyle within the provision God has supplied. When we are content to do this, God will always help us find a way.

### 5. KEEP A CLEAR CONSCIENCE.

Living with integrity means dealing with the past as well as the present. Part of becoming financially faithful requires gaining a clear conscience regarding past business practices and personal dealings. Sometimes, in addition to a changed attitude, our transformation means making restitution for situations where we have wronged someone.

Tim's story is a good example. Before he accepted Christ, he cheated someone out of some money. God convicted him about this and indicated that he should go and make restitution. He contacted the person, confessed what had been done, and offered to make it right. The person refused to forgive and also refused to take any money.

Tim's ego and pride were hurt until he realized that he had been both obedient and successful. His confession was not primarily for the offended person but for his own relationship with God. He had done exactly what God had asked, and God had forgiven him. Nothing further was required.

## 6. PUT OTHERS FIRST.

This does not imply being a door mat; it simply means that we shouldn't profit at the unfair expense of someone else. As is often the case, attitude is all-important.

## 7. MANAGE TIME PRIORITIES.

A workaholic might gain wealth at the expense of the family's relational needs, but wealth alone is no indicator of financial faithfulness. And wealth gained with wrong priorities is likely to vanish. *"Do not weary yourself to gain wealth, cease from your consideration of it. When you set your eyes on it, it is* gone. *For wealth certainly makes itself wings like an eagle that flies toward the heavens"* (Proverbs 23:4-5). Even if it doesn't vanish, it can't deliver the satisfaction it promises. Don't be deceived by overcommitment to business or the pursuit of wealth.

God's priorities for us are very clear.

**Priority number one** is to develop our relationship with Jesus Christ.

**Priority number two** is our family. This includes teaching them God's Word. And that requires quality time, something that can't exist without a sufficient quantity from which to flow.

Develop the habit of a regular time to study God's Word for yourself as well as a family time that acknowledges your commitment to each other and to God.

Turn off the television, have the children do their homework early, and begin to study the Bible together. Pray for each other and for those in need. Help your children become intercessors who can pray for others and expect God to answer.

**Priority number three** is your work, which God intends to be an opportunity for ministry and personal development in addition to providing an income.

**Priority number four** is church activities and other ministry. This does not imply that it is unimportant or can be neglected, but it keeps us from using church as an excuse to let higher priorities slide. If we observe priority number one, we will not neglect our church.

## 8. AVOID OVER-INDULGENCE.

Jesus said, *"If anyone wishes to come after Me, he must deny himself, and take up his cross daily and follow Me"* (Luke 9:23). Once again, this is about priorities. Who wins the contest between God's claim on your life and your own pursuit of pleasure?

In Philippians 3:18-19, Paul says that many live as the enemies of the cross of Christ, and he describes them by saying, *"Their destiny is destruction, their god is their stomach, and their glory is in their shame"* (NIV).

That sounds alarmingly like much of our culture, and it takes great effort to avoid being swept along with the current.

## 9. GET CHRISTIAN COUNSEL.

*"Without consultation, plans are frustrated, but with many counselors they succeed"* (Proverbs 15:22). God admonishes us to seek counsel and not to rely solely on our own resources. People are often frustrated in financial planning because they lack the necessary knowledge. A common but tragic response is to give up. Within the body of Christ, God has supplied those who have the ability to help in the area of finances. Seek Christian counselors.

To read more on what God says about handling money, go to Crown.org and click "Bible Tools."

# Crown's mission is to provide you with help, hope, and insight as you seek to grow in financial faithfulness.

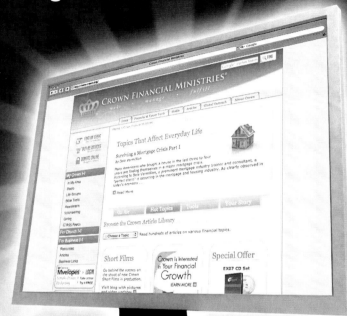

## Stay Connected at Crown.org

With a comprehensive collection of online tools and resources, Crown.org will teach you how to make money, manage money, and ultimately fulfill God's purposes for your life.

### God's wisdom will make a difference in your finances!

# *Giving You Help, Hope, and Insight!*

## MoneyLife™ Radio

### 3 WAYS MONEYLIFE™ CAN MAKE A DIFFERENCE IN YOUR FINANCES:

- Go deep on life issues that are confronting you on a daily basis
- Hear proven biblical financial principles and practical application
- Discover how making and managing money affects God's purposes for your life

### 3 WAYS TO LISTEN

- On-Air
- Online
- Podcast

## *Listen Now! Crown.org/Radio*

Chuck Bentley
Crown CEO and MoneyLife Host

# Resources

## To Help You in Life and Money

### Career Direct®

You have unlimited potential to be more, do more, and maximize your God-given talents and abilities. You are ready to exceed everyone's expectations.

**Go to CareerDirectOnline.org to get started.**

## Crown Budgeting Solutions

*Choose the Budgeting Solution That Fits Your Lifestyle*

### *Paper*

• Traditional option using paper, pen, and cash.

### *Software*

• Computer software option for your PC or Mac.

### *Online and Mobile*

• Web and Mobile option available anytime, anywhere.

**For details, go to Crown.org/BudgetingSolutions**